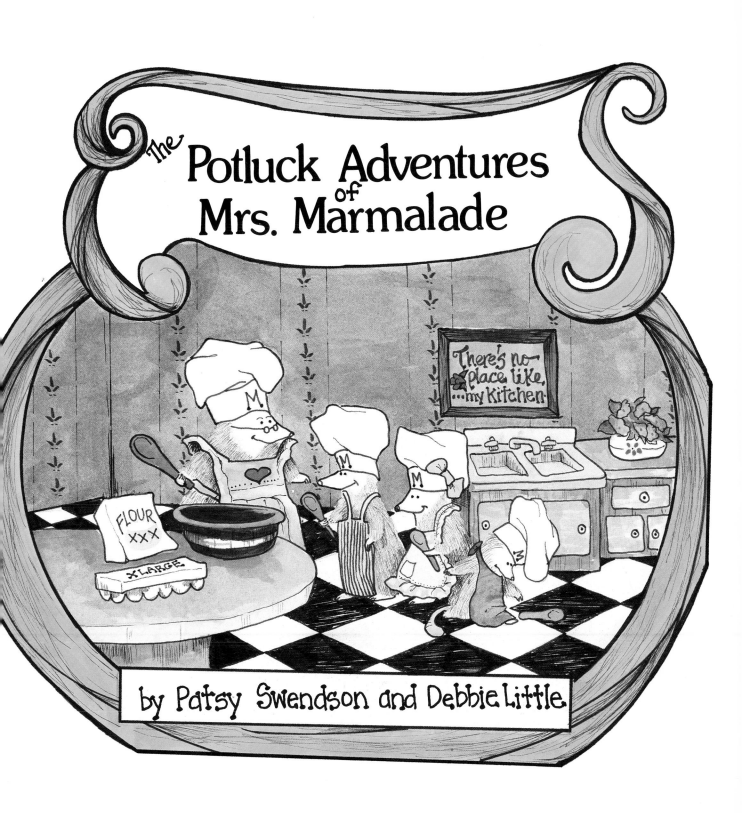

The Potluck Adventures of Mrs. Marmalade

There's no place like, ...my kitchen.

FLOUR XXX

XLARGE

by Patsy Swendson and Debbie Little

PANDA BOOKS

Kitchen Rules

All good cooks, whether possums or people, must follow simple kitchen rules:

1) Before cooking, put on an apron and wash your hands.
2) Always use a pot holder or oven mitts to handle hot pans or pots.
3) Always pick up a knife by its handle, not by its blade.
4) When you have finished cooking, make sure all oven and stove dials are turned OFF.
5) Always ask permission to use the kitchen and the ingredients.
6) Lift the lids of saucepans or casseroles away from you so the steam will not burn you.
7) Be sure your hands are dry when you plug in or disconnect any appliance.

To Aeri, my precious, precocious, and very special niece.

— AUNT PATSY

*For my nieces and nephews, Kristin, Stacy, Bradley and Bobby,
who are always in my heart.*

— AUNT DEBBIE

FIRST EDITION

Copyright © 1989
By Patsy Swendson and Debbie Little

Published in the United States of America
By Panda Books
An Imprint of Eakin Publications, Inc.
P.O. Drawer 90159   ★   Austin, TX 78709-0159

ISBN 0-89015-718-9

"What does she say? What does she say?" the children shouted.

"Just a minute," said Mrs. Marmalade. "It seems that Aunt Ibby is sick and she wants me to come help her."

"Make her better," the children cried. "Make Aunt Ibby smile again . . . Please!"

The very next day Mrs. Marmalade made plans to go to Aunt Ibby's. She made a list of rules to follow in the kitchen.

She hugged her children goodbye, knowing that they would be well cared for by the neighbor, Mrs. Smuggly.

"If you try to cook, be sure to ask her to help you. She knows a lot," she reminded them.

Mrs. Marmalade grabbed her satchel and started for the door. Slowly she turned to look at them and with a smile she said, "Just so that you won't forget me, I left a surprise for all of you in the kitchen."

Mrs. Marmalade's Surprise

Forget-Me-Not Cookies

Whites of two large eggs
$\frac{1}{4}$ t. cream of tartar
$\frac{2}{3}$ cups of sugar
1 6-oz. pkg. of chocolate chips
1 cup of chopped pecans
$\frac{1}{2}$ teaspoon of peppermint extract

Preheat oven to 350 degrees. Beat at room temperature egg whites with cream of tartar until soft peaks form. Gradually add the sugar, one tablespoon at a time until stiff peaks form. Fold in remaining ingredients with rubber spatula all at once.

Drop mixture by rounded teaspoon onto foil-lined cookie sheet. Place in oven; turn off oven immediately! Leave cookies overnight. Do not peek . . . not once!

After a few hours she came to a fork in the road.
"Which way do I go?" she asked.
"Which way do I go?" mocked a little bird on a tree stump.
"Who are you?" Mrs. Marmalade asked.
"Who are you?" the bird said.
Not wanting to play the mockingbird's game, Mrs. Marmalade decided to have a few snacks.

Adventure Snacks

Walking Salad

Take large, crispy lettuce leaves and in each one place a carrot stick, a celery stick, and a pickle slice. Wrap the lettuce around the vegetables and enjoy.

Salad in a Pocket

Yield: 2 servings

1 large pita bread round
Mayonnaise, for spreading
2 lettuce leaves
¼ cup tuna
1 T. sweet pickle relish
1 celery stalk, thinly sliced
1 slice of American cheese, halved

Cut the pita bread round in half. Carefully open the bread with your fingers so you can see the pocket in the bread. Spread the inside of the pocket with mayonnaise. Tuck a lettuce leaf into each one.

In a small bowl combine the tuna, relish, and celery. Spoon into each pocket. Place a slice of cheese in each. Enjoy.

As she finished her snacks, another bird approached her. This time it was a wise old owl whom she knew very well.

"Oh, Mr. Peabody, I'm so glad to see you. I'm on my way to see my Aunt Ibby in the city, and I'm not sure which road to take," Mrs. Marmalade said.

"Well, you will need to go that way," he replied. "But you must be thirsty. How about some lemonade?"

Mr. Peabody's Drink

Old-Fashioned Lemonade

Yield: 5 cups

- ¾ cup sugar
- 1 cup fresh squeezed lemon juice
- 4 cups cold water
- 1 lemon, thinly sliced

Combine sugar with the fresh lemon juice. Stir until sugar dissolves. Stir in water. Taste and add additional sugar to sweeten, if necessary. Serve in an ice cold pitcher with lots of ice cubes and lemon slices.

NOTE: You may use fresh limes instead of lemons.

When she finished her drink, Mrs. Marmalade continued on her journey. Before long she saw a squirrel carrying too many nuts.

"It would be easier if you carried less nuts," Mrs. Marmalade advised.

As the squirrel turned to see who was speaking, the nuts he was carrying fell to the ground.

"Now look what you made me do," mumbled Tumbleweed.

She pulled out a paper bag and helped him pick up the nuts. Then he walked off without even a proper "Thank you."

Tumbleweed's Sticky Rolls

Sticky Rolls

Yield: 12 rolls

2 T. honey
2 T. sugar
2 T. butter, softened
2 T. flour
1 pkg. "Heat and Serve" rolls
Pecan halves

Preheat oven to 375 degrees. In small mixing bowl, combine honey, sugar, butter, and flour. Place the rolls on a baking sheet and spread with the honey mixture. Arrange pecan halves on top of each roll. Bake about 15 minutes or until lightly browned. Serve hot.

"Hello there!" shouted Mr. Osgood the rabbit. He was hoeing in his garden. It was a beautiful garden.

Mrs. Marmalade rested on a wooden bench and admired Mr. Osgood's crops.

His chest puffed out with pride as he offered her a taste of his vegetable stew. He cooked it right in his garden.

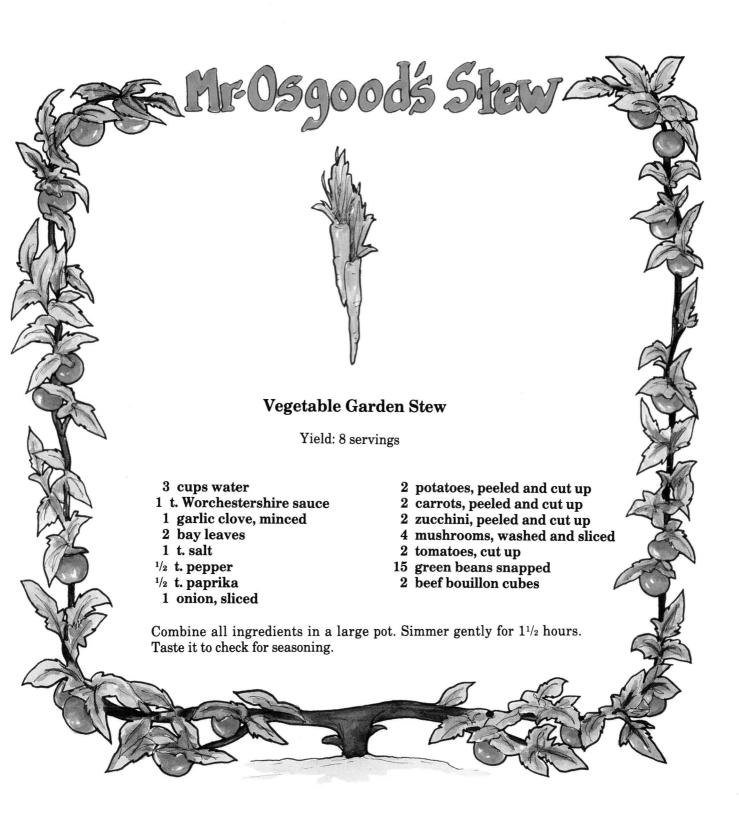

Mr. Osgood's Stew

Vegetable Garden Stew

Yield: 8 servings

3 cups water	2 potatoes, peeled and cut up
1 t. Worchestershire sauce	2 carrots, peeled and cut up
1 garlic clove, minced	2 zucchini, peeled and cut up
2 bay leaves	4 mushrooms, washed and sliced
1 t. salt	2 tomatoes, cut up
½ t. pepper	15 green beans snapped
½ t. paprika	2 beef bouillon cubes
1 onion, sliced	

Combine all ingredients in a large pot. Simmer gently for 1½ hours.
Taste it to check for seasoning.

She waved goodbye to Mr. Osgood and started on the trail again. She had gone up and down three hills when she heard some music and saw seven pigs dancing. It was a party!

"Come join the fun," shouted Hamlet Pig. "It's Hugh Mungo's birthday!"

Mrs. Marmalade danced and sang. She also ate a lot of goodies. What a good time they all had!

Party Treats

Happy Face Cupcake Cones

Yield: 24 servings

24 **flat-bottom ice cream cones**
 1 **pkg. Devil's Food Cake Mix**
 3 **large eggs**
¹/₂ **cup vegetable oil**
1¹/₃ **cups water**
Ice Cream

Preheat oven to 350 degrees. Set ice cream cones in small-cup muffin pans. Combine dry cake mix, eggs, oil, and water in large mixing bowl. Mix according to cake package instructions. Spoon 2 tablespoons batter into each cone.

Bake for 20–25 minutes or until a toothpick inserted in the center comes out clean. Cook on racks.

Top each cone with a scoop of ice cream. Create faces with M&M candies, coconut, red hot cinnamon candies, licorice, miniature marshmallows, and chocolate chips.

NOTE: Brownie mix may be used instead of the Devil's Food Cake Mix.

By this time, Mrs. Marmalade was very full and was walking very slowly. Suddenly, a wolf jumped out of the bushes. Mrs. Marmalade dropped her satchel and froze in her place.

Licking his lips, he said, "Don't you look delicious!"

From out of nowhere, an armadillo raced between them. Digger Armadillo stared the wolf straight in the eye. Because the wolf had never seen an armadillo before, he ran off. Mrs. Marmalade thanked Digger with a reward.

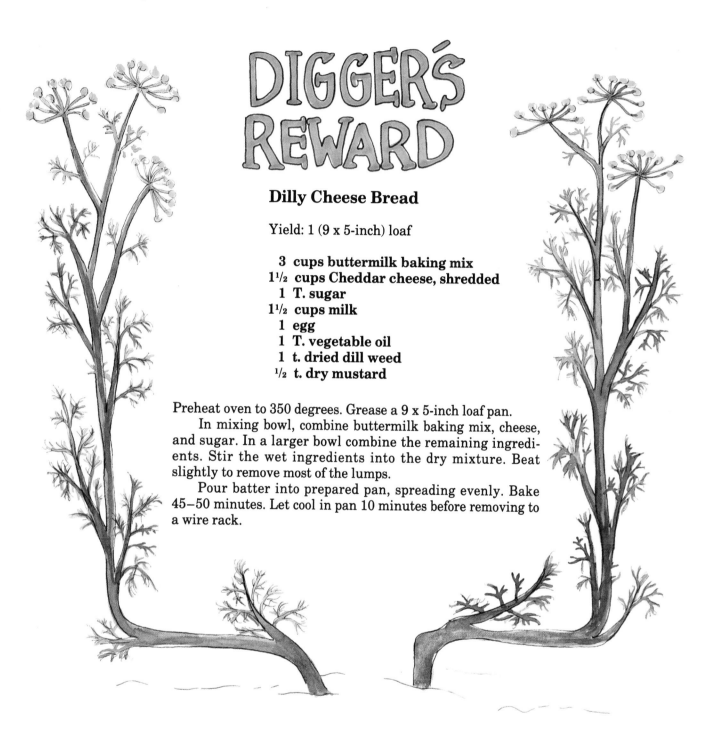

DIGGER'S REWARD

Dilly Cheese Bread

Yield: 1 (9 x 5-inch) loaf

- 3 cups buttermilk baking mix
- 1½ cups Cheddar cheese, shredded
- 1 T. sugar
- 1½ cups milk
- 1 egg
- 1 T. vegetable oil
- 1 t. dried dill weed
- ½ t. dry mustard

Preheat oven to 350 degrees. Grease a 9 x 5-inch loaf pan.

In mixing bowl, combine buttermilk baking mix, cheese, and sugar. In a larger bowl combine the remaining ingredients. Stir the wet ingredients into the dry mixture. Beat slightly to remove most of the lumps.

Pour batter into prepared pan, spreading evenly. Bake 45–50 minutes. Let cool in pan 10 minutes before removing to a wire rack.

Night was beginning to fall, so Mrs. Marmalade quickened her step. Raisin Giddings, her dearest and oldest friend, would be expecting her to spend the evening.

By the time she reached the house, Raisin was standing on the porch. The two hugged each other and talked non-stop from that moment well into the night.

In the morning, Raisin fixed Mrs. Marmalade a grand breakfast. The jam was especially good. As they said goodbye, they promised they would not wait so long to see each other again.

Good Morning

Raisin Giddings' Strawberry Jam

Thaw 2 pints of frozen strawberries. Mash with a fork or a potato masher. Add 3½ cups sugar and stir very well. Let mixture stand at room temperature for about 40 minutes. When the sugar is dissolved, add ½ bottle of liquid fruit pectin. Stir for 3 minutes. Pour into jars and cover. Refrigerate at least 24 hours before serving.

The city grew bigger the closer she got. So many things had changed since the last time she visited Aunt Ibby. But when she turned on 5th Street, Mrs. Marmalade felt calmer. Aunt Ibby's little pink house with the red geraniums in front looked quite familiar.

She let herself in and went straight to the kitchen to make some magic cinnamon tea. A large smile came to Aunt Ibby's face when she saw her niece carrying a silver tray.

Mrs. Marmalade's Cure

Magic Cinnamon Tea

Yield: 2 cups

2 cups water
2 tea bags
2 t. red hot cinnamon candies

Gently heat water until it begins to simmer. Pour into tea cups. Place a tea bag in each cup and let stand for 1–2 minutes. Remove bags and stir 1 teaspoon red hot cinnamon candies into each cup. Stir. Serve immediately.

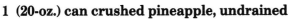

Out of the Dumps Cake

Yield: 12–16 servings

1 (20-oz.) can crushed pineapple, undrained
1 (21-oz.) can cherry pie filling
1 pkg. yellow cake mix
1 cup pecans, chopped
1 stick butter or margarine, cut into thin slices

Preheat oven to 350 degrees. Grease a 13 x 9 x 2-inch baking pan.

Spoon undrained pineapple into pan; spread evenly. Add pie filling and spread in even layer. Sprinkle dry cake mix onto cherry layer; spread evenly. Sprinkle pecans over cake mix. Place butter slices all over the top. Bake for 45–55 minutes. Serve warm or cold.

Sugar Toast (or Butterscotch Toast)

Yield: 2 servings

4 slices of bread
Butter
¹/₃ cup brown sugar
1 t. cinnamon

Lay the bread on a cookie sheet. Butter each slice. Sprinkle with brown sugar. Shake cinnamon onto each side. Place under preheated broiler just until bubbly and brown. Remove and cool slightly before eating.

Two days went by and Aunt Ibby started feeling much better.
Her friends, Clover and Honeysuckle, dropped by to see how she was
doing.

The two sisters brought their famous flower sandwiches.

"And you don't even have to water them," giggled Clover.

They spent a wonderful afternoon munching on sandwiches, sip-
ping hot apple cider, and telling stories they had all heard before.

Afternoon Break

Summery Flower Sandwiches

White or whole wheat sandwich bread
Cream cheese, softened
Hard-boiled eggs
 1 cucumber
 1 tomato
 4 parsley sprigs
 1 carrot
 ¼ cup tuna
 1 green onion

Cut the bread into 2- or 3-inch round shapes. Spread the rounds with softened cream cheese.

Arrange a flower design on each one. For example, make a daisy by cutting "petals" from the white of hard-boiled eggs. Sieve the yolk and use for the center of the flower. Use thin slices of cucumber or green onion tops for the stem and leaves.

Cut flowerpot shapes from tomato and use tuna for the blossoms and parsley for the leaves.

Use small cutters for the carrot to make flower shapes, again using green onion tops and cucumber for the stems and leaves.

NOTE: The very best part of this recipe is to use your imagination and come up with the prettiest flower sandwich you can think of. Get your friends to help make their own sandwiches. These are as much fun to make as they are to eat.

As much as Aunt Ibby wanted her favorite niece to stay, she knew Mrs. Marmalade had to get back to her children.

Aunt Ibby was feeling so good that she made a care package for Mrs. Marmalade to take home.

It is very special to have an aunt to love.

"Goodbye, Aunt Ibby," said Mrs. Marmalade. "Be sure to write us soon. Your letters always make us smile."

Aunt Ibby could not say a word. If she did, she knew she would cry.

Aunt Ibby's Care Package

Take-Along Mix 'Ems

1 cup roasted peanuts
1 cup seedless raisins
1 (6-oz.) pkg. chocolate chips
1 cup diced dried apple slices

Toss to combine. Store in a tightly closed container.

"Not to Eat" Play Dough

This is for making fun animals, creatures, anything . . . But it is **not to eat!**

1 cup flour
½ cup salt
2 t. cream of tartar
1 T. cooking oil
1 cup water
Food coloring, of your choice

Combine all dry ingredients in medium mixing bowl. In another bowl, combine oil, water, and food coloring. Add to dry ingredients and mix with a spoon.

Using a non-stick skillet, cook the mixture over medium-low heat until the mixture forms a large ball. (It will be a little lumpy.) Use a wooden spoon to stir the play dough in the skillet. Remove from heat and pour out onto waxed paper and knead until it is smooth and pliable. Store in an airtight container.

As Mrs. Marmalade left the city, she passed by the beach. Although she was eager to get home, she decided to relax in the sun and enjoy the sounds of the water.

Two muscle-bound sea gulls, Lou and Hank, stopped by to say hello.

"Nice day," said Lou.

"Very nice day," said Hank.

"A very super nice day," answered Mrs. Marmalade.

Since they were all in agreement, Lou and Hank offered Mrs. Marmalade some sand tart cookies they were carrying in a bag.

"At the Coast" Cookies

Sand Tarts

Yield: 4 dozen cookies

      1 **cup butter or margarine, softened**
    $^1/_2$ **cup powdered sugar**
      1 **t. vanilla**
   2$^1/_4$ **cups flour**
    $^1/_4$ **t. salt**
    $^3/_4$ **cup finely chopped pecans**
Additional powdered sugar

Heat oven to 400 degrees. Combine butter, powdered sugar, and vanilla. Stir in flour, salt, and nuts until mixture holds together. Shape dough into 1-inch balls.

   Place on ungreased baking sheet. Bake 10–12 minutes or until set, but not brown. While still warm, roll in powdered sugar. Cool. Roll again in powdered sugar.

Once again Mrs. Marmalade was on the road leading home. The river ahead meant she was close to home. She smiled as she saw the two fat and lazy river cats, Pedernales and Fern. After another unsuccessful morning of fishing, they were making-do with hot dogs again.

Because they had never caught a fish in their lives, they were experts at hot dogs. So Mrs. Marmalade decided to join them for lunch.

Fishermen's Advice

Popsicle Hot Dogs

10 frankfurters
10 popsicle sticks
10 buns
Relishes and sauces to taste

Push popsicle sticks into frankfurters, leaving 3–4 inches of the stick protruding. Grill on rack, turning often. The sticks allow for easy turning on the grill and easy eating. Serve on buns with relishes and sauces.

Lazy Day Hot Dogs

Yield: 4 servings

4 slices of bread
Butter or margarine, for spreading
³⁄₄ cup minced parsley
4 hot dogs, sliced lengthwise in halves
¹⁄₂ cup mayonnaise
1 T. chili sauce
1 t. prepared yellow mustard

Spread each slice of bread with butter or margarine. Dip the buttered side of the bread into minced parsley to cover each slice. Place 2 hot dog slices, skin side down, on each piece of bread.

In a small bowl, combine mayonnaise, chili sauce, and yellow mustard. Pour over hot dogs, leaving ends of hot dogs uncovered. Place on a baking sheet in a 450-degree oven for 5–7 minutes. Serve immediately.

Exhausted from her trip, Mrs. Marmalade approached her house. She opened the door and was delighted to see the banner stretched across the wall. Then the smell of her favorite strawberry bread filled the room.

What wonderful children she had! She had missed them terribly.

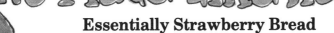

No Place Like Home

Essentially Strawberry Bread

    1 cup sour cream
    1 cup strawberry jam
    1 cup butter, softened
1½ cups sugar
    4 eggs
    3 cups flour
    1 t. baking soda
¾ t. cream of tartar
    1 t. lemon extract
    1 t. vanilla
½ cup pecans, chopped
Powdered sugar

In small mixing bowl, fold sour cream into jam. In large mixing bowl, cream butter and sugar together until smooth; add eggs, beating well. Add jam mixture alternately with flour, soda, and cream of tartar. Stir in lemon and vanilla extracts and the chopped pecans. Bake in greased 10-inch tube pan or in 2 loaf pans in a 325-degree oven for 1 hour or until a toothpick inserted in the center comes out clean. Cool slightly; remove from pan. When cool, sprinkle with powdered sugar.

GOODNITE TO ALL

Hugs

²/₃ cup butter, softened
1 cup sugar
1 t. vanilla
½ t. almond extract
1 egg
1 T. milk
2½ cups flour
1½ t. baking powder
¾ t. salt
2 cups 'quick' oats
Miniature chocolate chips

In mixing bowl, beat butter, sugar, vanilla, and almond extract until light. Add egg and milk; beat until fluffy. Combine flour, baking powder, and salt. Blend into creamed mixture. Stir in oats. chill dough 1½ hours.

Roll dough to 1/8-inch thickness between two sheets of waxed paper. Cut into "bear" shapes. Press chocolate chips into each cookie to form eyes and buttons. Bake on greased cookie sheets in a 375-degree oven for 8–10 minutes. Cool slightly before removing from pans. When completely cooled, add a red frosting "smile."

That night everyone snuggled together on the couch in their nightgowns. They sipped on herbal tea sweetened with honey as Mrs. Marmalade told them of her adventures. When she was done, she gave them a hug.

"I had a good time," she said, "but nowhere on earth would I rather be than here with you."